# Still Being Refreshed:

# Memoir of the Refresher

*My Life is not a fairytale*

**Tonya Woodridge-Jarvis**

# Dedication

This book is dedicated to my loving husband for allowing me to use our personal lives as a platform for helping other individuals.

I will always love and cherish you!

# Introduction

In my first book, The Refresher's Course, I was vague on some situations. So in this book I will clear up any questions that my readers may have. My readers have been asking for more and so here is the full throttle of the Refresher. Don't be alarmed, some of the stories are the same, but there is a more in-depth explanation of the encounters, where the previous reader may have had questions.

I will go on to warn you that some of the stories in this book may be a little unorthodox for some. But I am hoping that the book will save, heal and/or touch someone's life so that they may give their lives over to Christ.

I found that everyone is not happy for your projects and there will be naysayers everywhere you turn. But keep moving; follow your dreams, signs and wonders until the manifestation comes.

God is pleased by the obedience and purity of heart. I was just brave enough to write about ours.

# The Beginning

I am a young country girl in the "Sticks" of Jackson, La raised primarily by her father's grandmother. I have two siblings, one of which I shared the womb with, and an older sister.

We all lived together for quite some time, the kids, my grandmother, grandfather, my mother, my father and my Uncle Jethro. It was good clean ciaos all the time.

My parents moved into their own place in McManus, a little town in Jackson, La of which we were still surrounded by family. We would play outside for hours on end with no worries or cares. My mother would dress us up like magazine dolls. Her children were her pride and joy. But some changes were approaching rapidly.

Shortly after the move, I remember the death of my grandfather which really took a toll on my brother. They were thick as thieves. He had him driving at the age of nine. My grandfather would take up for him, but not spare the rod when he needed to.

Meanwhile, my mother and father are going through tough times right now. I could hear them belittle and degrading each other. One day we were asked to walk up the street to an older cousin's house (of which whom told everyone's business, but her own) because of an altercation they were having. I can remember them arguing and her leaving to go out to a night club. This one particular time, it was raining pretty badly and she wanted us to stay at her mother's house, but her mother, my grandmother, stated that my sister could stay and let her inside the house and left my brother and I in the rain. You would think she (my mother) would have caught an attitude and said, if one can't stay than the other can't stay either. Nope. She didn't. She left my sister anyways and found another cousin for my brother and me. After many moons of arguments and fighting my mother moved my siblings and I to Baker, La.

My sister and I were strong enough to endure the move; however, my brother took a turn for the worst. He was feeling like our father abandoned him and that our mother didn't love him. He began a string of crimes, running away from home and being put in and out of the jail system for many years.

My father has acquired an addition to the family, a wife and daughter. My brother was sent to live with him and his new family but only for a moment.

So now it is just the two of us, my sister and me. However, some things aren't completely right on the home front. My sister is on a pedestal of some kind, but no one seems to think so, but me and my mother is full of strong drink all the time. The majority of my first cousins kept us for several nights while my mother was partying. When my mother would come to pick us up in the wee hours of the morning, full of strong drink, we would get into countless accidents, but she was so persuasive, that the police always let her go.

But a grandmother's love goes a long way. This woman had phenomenal faith of which I am sure didn't come overnight. I couldn't wait until the weekend, which was the time I spent at my grandmothers. She always welcomed me with open arms. She had several rules but the ones that seem to always stick out are: have a relationship with God, keep the kitchen, living room and bathrooms cleaned at all times and don't roll stone for stone.

We would go to church on Sundays, Mondays, Wednesdays and the business meetings on Thursdays. I was present at vacation bible school and anything extra she signed me up for because I didn't have a choice in the matter. My grandmother was a soldier in the army of the Lord and she made sure that I was as well willingly or unwillingly.

She would cook like it was a holiday every Sunday. She made sure that I was near her and I wanted to be, watching her every move to learn all of her cooking tricks and secrets. She grew a lot of her own vegetables and O how I hated the bugs in the garden, but did as I was told. I was learning work ethic and non existence excuses at a young age.

Everyone would stop by on Sundays for dinner. I didn't mind getting up at 5am to clean and cook even though she wasn't going to allow me to touch anything, she just wanted my company. It was ok; I knew it would all pay off in the end or at least I was hoping.

My life would go on like this for years. Until one day we as in my sister and I are being uprooted again. The next four years of my life would change drastically.

We now live in Zachary, La and my brother is back (another form of rejection in his life) and we are all going to high school. We also have some new additions to our family. I have now acquired a stepfather, two stepsisters and a Cajun step-grandmother. We are all trying to mesh well with the unexpected blended family. There were some bumps in the road, between the younger stepsister and my siblings but we swiftly learned the concept of getting along or getting a beating or punished.

Over the next few years, my high school years, constant changes would happen. The relationship with my mother was on a fast paced roller coaster spiraling into downward plunge, her relationship with my stepfather was diminishing and my brother was growing further away from reality. On top of that my sister was being placed on a pedestal like the Statue of Liberty. Of course, my brother noticed it as well. He had begun to do things to gain attention and the same affection given to the Statue of Liberty. He had so much anger built up inside of him. We were fellowshipping at a lackluster church stuck in tradition who couldn't cast out anything that he had on the inside of him. So he was labeled and not helped.

I remember the family traveling to a Southern University football game in Jackson, Ms, when the neighbors called to say that our house was on fire. That morning, before we left for travel, my brother, apparently trying to calm his nerves before a car ride with the entire family, put a lit cigarette in his dresser drawer which ignited the clothes and engrossed our home in flames. By the time we arrived home, several rooms were gone and other articles were unsalvageable. Of course the rapture came that night and he had to go.

So my brother is gone now and I am next in line to work on her nerves. My inner self and I often toyed with the idea of what is her problem with me. Is there a deep dark, dank secret that I don't know about?

My mother and I would have these horrible arguments. She would always point out how I wasn't going to make it in life and of course tried to select my friends of whom she thought would be better for me. She criticized me for my diction and the way I carried myself. She would ask me if I was putting on heirs. I didn't even know what that meant at the time. But I was just being Tonya. I remember how she would back hand me across the face if I didn't agree with something she said or if she was wrong about something and I quickly pointed it out. It was foreseen as me being smart. I saw it as just merely stating the facts.

My grades had started to slip and I knew that failure wasn't an option. That would prove that she was right about me all along. One day I just decided to leave because I couldn't take it anymore, I figured she didn't care anyway. I went to stay at a friend's house and went to school from there. I started bringing my grades up and felt like things were looking up, then my stepfather shows up, tells me to come home and I did as I was told. But in the back of my mind, I knew she (my mother) didn't want me there, nor was she worried about me being gone.

So I'm back at the home front with the same drama. I've quietly been doing a countdown to graduation. That summer, my mother signed me up for a summer job of which she lied on my application, because I wasn't old enough. I purchased all of my school clothes, my senior stuff and my sister's. I didn't mind because I had a choice in what I purchased which ticked her off. Once that job came to an end, I quickly found another.

It's high school graduation time. I graduated on time, despite the naysayers. I was taken to dinner but could not invite any of my friends or go to any parties. On top of that, my sister, who graduated after me, received a car and I did not. My mother never taught me how to drive, where to purchase a driver's license, take the driver's education class or get a state id for that matter. Once again, my sister is on a pedestal. I didn't get my license until the age of 23.

Not to mention right after graduation, Caution: My sister was being groomed for Greatness! My aunt set her up with not just a job but a career where she could work her way up the ladder, had an excellent benefit package as well as other perks. I often questioned why I wasn't given the same opportunity. Am I not good enough? So I lived by my own set of rules and made my own plans.

We have not always been awarded the same opportunities in life, but God groomed me for greatness and that's who I shall be!

The Refresher

I moved out shortly after graduation and got an apartment with my boyfriend of whom I had been friends with since the seventh grade. I was doing well and being grown. As a direct result of my doing well and being grown, I became pregnant at the age of nineteen with my first child and the first grandchild on both sides. I hid the pregnancy for a while before I told my mother. I was afraid of what she was going to say. But in small towns nothing is ever a secret.

I finally made the phone call to tell her. She was so harsh and demeaning to me. She said that I was out running the streets with different men. My inner self was like "she knows this boy and his family". We grew up right down the street in Jackson together. I was literally crushed. Then my son's father announces that he is going to the Navy. So with no income of my own, I needed a plan.

My stepdad asked me to return home to make sure that I was getting the proper prenatal care that I needed. He and my mom weren't on good terms at all. They are not sleeping in the same bedroom. Not to mention when I arrived, I'm four months pregnant and had to sleep on the sofa because my sister didn't want to share her bedroom with me. My stepdad took me to a job interview because I wasn't showing at the time; I received the job at Wal-Mart. I'm thinking things are really looking up now.

As my belly grew bigger, my mother grew bitter. My stepdad started staying away from the house. When he would leave, he would wake me up to get in their bed. My mother was furious because he cared. One day I went to work in November of 1999, and came home to an empty place, where my mother had moved out, took my sister and left me. And to add insult to injury, she left two plates, two forks, two spoons, two cups, and all of my pictures.

She left no forwarding information, and not to mention my son's father had just gotten married in the Navy and that my son also has a brother that is four months older than he is. I'm pissed and quite ready to go off.

"The devil has a way of making you think that you can't go on without making illegitimate excuses and being wrapped up, tangled up and bogged down in sin and promiscuity. "
The Refresher

I was confused because how could a mother leave her child. I later found out a rumor that she was telling everyone, she said "I thought that you didn't want to go", but told family members that the child that I was carrying was for my stepdad. I couldn't believe what happened, but I needed to keep going. Its December 1999, a bouncing baby boy arrived with no grandmother at the hospital. My inner-self was still hoping for a miracle. My stepdad and I started having these arguments about who could be at the house. I figured if I am paying half, then we are roommates. So I filed my tax return, found an apartment and moved out. I have this child that I'm trying to care for and I can't get a ride to work. I ended up losing my job at Wal-Mart. At this point, I need a hustle plan.

All bills had a different man assigned to them. I learned bookkeeping at an early age. But when I stopped, the money stopped coming in. My son is four months now, and I can't continue to pay the bills, buy diapers and feed us both. I remember having to put T-shirts around his bottom because there was no money for diapers. I remember thinking about giving up on my life and his.

I had to make oatmeal with a coke because the water was turned off. And on top of all of that I had received an eviction notice. With no money and no supposed friends, where will I end up with this kid? I don't want to leave him like my mother did me. Lord, please help me!

I started researching programs for homeless teens. I found one that interviewed me and allowed me to go through the screening process. I prayed like never before. I wanted to change my life around and figured that this could be the way. I was scared and nervous as hell. But I knew that a hustle plan was a priority.

I was given a mentor and she did an excellent job. She told me that I could be anything that I wanted and she would show me how. The program issued a furnished apartment, free daycare and an allowance of which needed to budgeted for the week. The rules were simple, you have eighteen months to get your life in order after that we cut you off.

I immediately enrolled in an eighteen month college program and started a work-study job. I would walk and catch the bus, because of the apartment location; the bus route was a mile away. The free day care services weren't on the route either. So I would walk to take my son to daycare first, leave his stroller there and then walk another half mile to catch my bus to school, stay after for work study then repeat the process in the evening, rain, sleet or snow. Sometimes the walk would be six miles or longer because of no bus fare. I remember walking and talking to God. I would tell myself a story of how it was going to get better for us.

My mentor, then approached me to ask if I would be interested in traveling to promote homeless teen and runaway youth awareness. I was elated to do so. I begin to travel all over the globe, facilitating meetings with senators and was even featured in a video promoting homeless teen and runaway youth awareness. God had his hand on my life and I didn't know it.

Then things were shaken up a bit because the mentor I had received a promotion and I was then given a male mentor. What the hell? Of course I bucked at the system because I didn't want a male. I knew what I was capable of.  Once again that relationship didn't last long at all. She (my original mentor) then returned just to work with me. She couldn't understand, why there was a "disconnect" with him and me.

I later explained to her that men were tools for me; I use them to fix what I needed and then placed them back in the garage for safe keeping until the next go around. So the male mentor with all of his book sense sure as hell wasn't going to change anything but walk into the silent but deadly trap that was set for him.

I received word that my grandmother was ill. I wasn't able to go and see her like I wanted to because of the location she was in and lack of transportation on my part. So my inner self was at odds trying to cope with the situation.

Although prayers and hospital visits weren't enough to keep her here, she was called home to be with the Lord. I can remember sitting at her funeral numb to the touch.

The death of my grandmother really took a toll on my life. Is this another person leaving me? I didn't want to go on. I don't care about school or anything else. I wanted her to at least see me do something good for myself. I would say to her spirit, I can do better! I could hear her voice saying" I'm here and always will be."

"The change that I want and need to see must first begin me." The Refresher

My grades started to decline in school. The administrators from the college placed me academic probation. I went from a 3.4 to 1.5 GPA in a matter of weeks. They basically told me that I could lose my financial aid if I didn't get my act together.

Hard work pays off. It is graduation day from college. I did something good for myself, stuck with it and it is finally paying off. I walked across the stage proudly and in tears as I looked into the audience and the only person that was there was my mentor. There were no friends and no family. Has she (my mother) turned everyone against me? I sent out invites. I quickly learned the concept of everybody you hang with and think that you are close to, isn't necessarily happy for you.

The program came to an end. And my mentor was no more. Who will keep me in line? This is yet another person, I have to let go of? People keep leaving me. I must admit I became a little discouraged and depressed. I realize now that people are placed in your life for reasons, seasons and lifetimes. They all will fall under at least one of those categories.

I was finished with school and finished with the program. I am working and just trying to make ends meet. I ended up having to put my son into a 24-hour daycare because of the hours that I was working. My son became stressed as a baby and he began to break out in hives because he had separation anxiety. He later developed a sleeping disorder. I knew that this was my fault because he went from being right under me all the time to being in a 24-hour daycare not having his mother around. I was still trying to do what was right by my son. I blamed myself for a while, but what was I to do.

My mother then finds out that my son was in a 24-hour daycare and told me to give him to her because I wasn't rearing him well. I was completely floored. My inner-self was like; She could have asked me if I needed help with him, she had a multiplicity of folks, a village if you will, helping her to raise us. But that day, I made a promise to myself and to God that I will train my child up in the way that he should go in Jesus name.

We would not speak for several years after that. I would move around a lot trying to create a life for the both of us. I tried to reconnect with her to do my part, but it hasn't happened as of yet. But I trust God. She says nice things about me and compliments me to other people, but never to me. I still keep my connection alive on my end. I send messages every now and again. All I can do is my part. It's funny because I struggle with situations when people ask me how she is doing and I have to lie and ask for forgiveness because the truth of the matter is, I really don't know.

But a simple: Tonya, I am proud of you for straightening your life up. You've managed to get an education, become successful, take care of yourself, stay out of jail, be drug free, and take care of your family. It must be too hard to ask for!

The Refresher

I didn't and don't bad mouth her to my kids; I made excuses when they were younger. My older son is happy with whatever comes his way, but the youngest one is highly analytical and wants answers. So I allowed him to call and investigate to satisfy his interest. But there was no answer.

I needed to cut down on the hours that I was working to be with my son. So I began to give plasma, as though it was my second job, to make ends meet. I literally looked like I did drugs with track marks on my arms. I found out that you can go to all the centers as long as you didn't go to an affiliate where your name would already be in the system. I remember this one particular time, when my menstrual cycle was on, I went to give plasma, I became so weak, but any sign of weakness, they can't do it and you wouldn't be paid for that session. I nearly passed out, but kept a straight face, I needed the money. I rode the bus home, and the bus driver asked me if I was ok, and I told him yes. Needless to say, I fainted when I got to my apartment door. I knew this baby couldn't survive without me.

# The Turning

It would be two years before I even took a man seriously. I met a friend of a friend who was a chef at the time. We started dating. We became engaged in six month's time and he purchased me a car from the showroom floor of which had his name on it, because I didn't have a license, and now I'm planning a wedding. After the wedding his family wanted to buy a trailer and put on their property for us. But two months before the wedding I found out that I was pregnant. So everything is moving along and I am now planning for a wedding, a baby and a move at the same time. I then had a miscarriage. But he not knowing how to deal with a situation of this magnitude went to work, while I had a D&C done. So I went through the process and didn't tell a soul. Two weeks after my procedure, he wanted to have sex. Of course I said no, because it wasn't time yet. So he tried to take it. After turning myself into a well defined "Incredible Hulk", he quickly told me that he was leaving. I then told my family that the wedding was off! I ended up telling about the entire situation. But my mother (who only shows up to show off and wanted to wear her specially made suit with a tail on it) tracks down the boy's family to see what happened and if it could be fixed. Whhaaatttt!! I was fit to be tied. Why did I need to be married so soon, it wasn't like she was taking care of me?

I'm trying this dating again. I befriended a guy and wasn't really trying to start ANY type of relationship. I just wanted to be friends. We would hang out like I was one of the guys. One night after drinking and clubbing, we slept together and Dangit! I became pregnant with bouncing boy number (2). What? I don't want any more children. He later told me that he had done that on purpose. He begged and pleaded with me to have the child. I declined for months. I was taking pills to make my period come on, meaning if you catch the pregnancy early enough it will cause you to miscarry. The pills weren't working for me. So I needed another plan. My inner self and I were at war because I wanted money for an abortion. My bed was already hard and I wasn't attempting to bring another child in the world that I solely can't take of. I was into to depending on me and not depending on God to see us through. Keep in mind at this point; trusting people to stick around was not one of my stronger qualities. And I wasn't sure that I wanted him to. Dang! My inner self won.

I decided to go through with the pregnancy and by this time we are engaged. This is all moving rather quickly and I am trying to wrap my head around it. However, I am moving forward with it because I don't want to become another statistic, adding to the bastard child collection.

In my eighth month of pregnancy and planning a wedding, I found out he (soon to be husband) had a child that was four months older than my son. I kept going and I still married him. We had a medium sized wedding that didn't last no longer than John stayed in the army of which, according to the old folks wasn't very long at all.

We were both young and not ready to grow up. He thought that fighting was the answer to solving problems. He was battling several things and not to mention he was after his mother's heart, not mine. Our last big blow up before I left was a wake up call because I could have and wanted to kill him that day. It was like he had single handily turned me into a FOOL.

Over the next couple of days, I would search around for apartments. I found one and told the manager MY story. She gave me the apartment key and said that I could move in. With no help, I made several trips back and forth to move our things (the boys and I) into the new apartment. The only items, I took were the kid's bedroom furniture and my clothes. I didn't even have a bed.

Months would go by as I started to attempt to rebuild myself and let go of the past. I didn't hear from him and was under the impression that he didn't know where we had moved to. Unbeknown to me, he'd been following me to get the location of the apartment.

One night, I decided to have a friend over. He (the soon to be ex husband) shows up with two guns like Rambo from an action movie, and breaks into the apartment through the window. He shoots at my friend, of which had to jump out of the second story window, the bullet lands in a house across the street and behind the apartment complex in a little girl's bedroom mattress. Speechless! I am looking at all of this in shock, but couldn't move, nor scream. I became so calm at this point. My children were in their rooms sleeping and didn't wake up to any of this. Thank God! He (soon to be ex husband) comes back to where I was standing and waves the gun at me and says "If I can't have you then no one else will either" I said "Well kill me right now because I don't want you. This is not what I want for our lives." He dropped his head and walked away. Shortly after the incident, he was put in jail and I filed for divorce. I didn't want anything from him except all rights to my son (bouncing baby boy 2).

# Relief

Hurricane Katrina happened and I started a new job that came with several new opportunities. I was given another impromptu mentor which changed my life yet again. She asked me one simple question, "Why are you so angry?" She said "you have everything it takes to be so successful, but your attitude stinks." I never realized that people saw me that way. I wasn't trying to be angry, I just had unfinished cooped up mental anguish that was seeping out every once in a while. But I wanted to change. I figured if she believed in me, why couldn't I. She began to talk to me and scold me when I was incorrect, which was the majority of the time. She provided me with a multiplicity of direction on a personal and professional level. She was another one of God's angels placed in my path.

She also showed me how to release some of that pent up bitterness. We would go to church together and have spiritual conversations on a regular basis. She gave me promotions of which I thought I couldn't handle, but she saw potential in me. Some of my so-called friends begin to pass me by and dwindle away. The job assignment was now coming to an end and she (my impromptu mentor) had to leave. What the hell? Yet another person leaving. So now I'm learning not to value or hold on to anything or anybody or at least I thought.

"Picking scabs can cause you to bleed uncontrollably unless you heal them completely."

The Refresher

This quote simply means that healing properly needs to take place before moving on. Sometimes we move on and there is still hurt there and we carry over to other situations and when something similar happens, we result back to what we are accustomed to, because we haven't fully let it go/healed or even forgiven in the past.

# Trusting?

I am growing spiritually and mentally at this point. I was really just attempting to keep my head above water. My older son started to rebel because he was trying to figure out why his father didn't want to be a part of his life. My inner self wanted to just give him the bare blunt of the truth. However, I refrained and just told him that he was working. He (my older son) would call, sit and wait for him (his father) to come of which he never showed. That pissed me off. You can do or say whatever you like to me but don't bother my boys. Years of this mental anguish would go on and my son would rebel every time. I made the decision to have a vividly devastatingly open, candid conversation with him (my oldest son's father), stating that either "you will sign up for full-time because part-time is not gone work! I will tell my son that you moved to Dubai."

Of course, I always had to clean up situations that he (my oldest son's father) promised. But I never bad mouthed him in the front of my child. I would just go into DEEP prayer. I learned to deal with the situations as they came and made him accountable. I allowed my son to deal directly with him so he can love his father, but see his father for what and who  he truly was.

As a single parent, they is no room for "I don't have it." I have to provide no matter what. It is all on me. I don't get any breaks. I'm  a mother, a doctor, a maid, the cook, the bookkeeper, the lawn care worker, a tutors and not to mention whatever profession that I  may have at the time, and this is all in one household.

Young males need stronger male figures in their lives and vice versa. So it is time to get up, dust myself off and get back into the dating pool.

Time has passed and I wasn't thinking about a relationship. I wanted to reestablish my relationship with the Lord and take care of my boys. I had been hurt entirely too many times. I had given up on finding love or even allowing it to come near me at this point.

I was riding with a co-worker/friend, who says "I need to stop by my brother's house for a second." Her brother says "who's your friend." At this point I am giving major attitude, right, because I don't want to be bothered. He (the brother) says "can I call you sometime." I said "No." So I wouldn't see him for a couple of months and then there was a party for the kids and he was there. Why, I don't know because he didn't even have any small children. He asked for my number again and I obliged. We would talk on the phone for hours at a time. He became my best friend. He would send me flowers to work and really had his romance game on point. But I just didn't want a relationship him. I really didn't want to be close with anyone.

He never wanted anything that I didn't want or at least he said. I knew in his mind, we were already in a relationship and married. He has asked me to marry him several times. I declined. He told me that he loved me and he knew I loved him; of course I wouldn't ever admit it. I think I loved him as a good down to earth friend.

God has a way of humbling you and making you adhere to his voice. I was on a job making $50,000/a year, which was good enough for me and the boys. My friend felt like he was voted out of the picture because I didn't need him anymore. Two days before my birthday, I was called in for a meeting, fired and not given any reasoning behind it. I was simply devastated. I didn't tell my friend, right away.

I was at church, one Sunday, and the Lord spoke to me, He said "That's your husband". I was like, Really? My inner self and I are at war because I know my track record and this can't be good. But I was obedient and I went straight to his house after that church service and told him that we were getting married and he said ok. I wanted him to say No, because it was like I was marrying him for convenience and I didn't want that to be the case. I went on giving him the details of the wedding and he complied. I was truly expecting him to say no. Because he was not my choice but he was God's choice for me. Again, a baby in Christ is not always prone to stand on His word.

I later found out that he knew that convenience and circumstance played a big factor in my marriage decision to him. I also found out that he had a bit of circumstance in there as well but will never admit it. I asked him why he went along with it. He said that he loved me and has been in love with me since day one. He said that he used to pray at night for God to remove me from his life. He already had a revelation. He was just waiting on me with the manifestation. He (my soon to be husband) accepted me with ALL of my faults and foolery.

I gave many stipulations on the marriage almost trying to control/manipulate the situation to run him off and he shall not be moved, didn't and hasn't. He was smoking and drinking, which all that all had to cease. I had several hang-ups with drinking, judging from some of my previous stories. He was a bit overweight, a fossil in my opinion at the time and that just wasn't good enough. He didn't care and agreed to all of these things no matter how ignorant they seemed. He was quite persistent, no matter how obtuse I was. He remained patient with me. He is not what I imagined, but I will abide by any decision that I make. How dare I want him to be perfect because I sure as hell wasn't by far? We laugh about it now; he jokingly says "most people wouldn't have stayed so I know God has played a BIG role in this marriage."

I also found out that the smoking and drinking was years of mental anguish and a family trait that had been instilled in him since birth, which is something that can't be broken overnight. I stopped nagging him about it and he stopped on his own. (Several praying nights) Sometimes we as women can drive men to do things by the way we react to them.

Men are gentle giants and all they need is motivation and a vast amount of encouragement from us as their wives and vice versa. When we go out into the world with different people/spirits every day, people are constantly pulling from us at every turn, so when we come home, the spouse's job is to build us up again, so that we may conquer the world again tomorrow and be able to do that with a clean slate.

**Rule of Thumb**: A rule that helps us to deal with arguments; you have 20 seconds to get your feelings out or vent if you will. After those 20 seconds that is it. The situation is in the rear view mirror which means that it is in the past and it is time to move on.

I later apologized for not giving him the uncompromiseable and unconditional love that he deserved.

Studies have shown that if you can make it within the first three years of marriage, you just may be built for it. The first three years of marriage are the hardest. You try to pack up and leave every other argument. Build a foundation. This means to seek God first, be humble, give accountability, motivate and encourage, keep the lines of communication open, always recharge your relationship, have patience and compassion for and with each other, don't over-react to situations, become selfless instead of selfish and just apologize.

Most importantly, don't allow your words to cut so deep. Sometimes those simple words out of anger can rip someone's soul away from them and they won't be able to recover from that.

**Rule of Thumb:** Watch how you relay messages in anger.

# No Patience?

The Lord is my shepherd; I shall not want. He maketh me to lie down in green pastures: he leadeth me beside the still waters. He restoreth my soul: he leadeth me in the paths of righteousness for his name's sake. Yea, though I walk through the valley of the shadow of death, I will fear no evil: for thou ART with me; thy rod and thy staff they comfort me. Thou preparest a table before me in the presence of mine enemies: thou anointest my head with oil; my cup runneth over. Surely goodness and mercy shall follow me all the days of my life: and I will dwell in the house of the LORD forever. Psalm 23.

But I'm in hell.  Am I refreshed? Is there a constant refreshing process?  The stresses of marriages, kids and jobs are gainfully working my nerves and Lord knows I'm trying not to miss the mark; I am trying to get into heaven. Hell is real and I am not trying to go. I want to be saved and live a righteous life, but at every turn sin is present and popular.

One night I decided to unwind by going out to eat. As I'm sitting there having a war with my inner self, I see someone staring at me. He asked if he could join me. I obliged. We laughed and talked for hours. We talked about our crazy childhoods, likes and dislikes. We even discussed our futuristic goals in life. I was in complete shock because; I'm thinking, where did he come from? To intrigue me like this. I am normally the dominant one, always in control and can handle countless sticky situations like this.

But ok, I'm thinking I'm in a lackluster relationship anyway. I can bite. What could it hurt? So the restaurant is closing down, we are walking to our respective vehicles. He asks me for my number to set up a lunch date, I hesitate at first, and then I give in. But oh no, I couldn't stop there. He walked me to my car and then I walked him to his. Then I stop him midway and kissed him like I had kissed no one before. My inner self was having a blast and a breakdown all at the same time.

So I walked to my car, sprinting really, trying to figure out what the hell did I just do. I'm sitting in my car, he pulls up on the side of me and says, I want to make sure you get home safe; I'll follow you half way. I was like, ok. My inner self is having so many thoughts of how this night is going to turn out. He did as he said the halfway point. I kept checking my rearview mirror to be sure.

I get home and I'm having a war with my emotions because I felt defeated. I should have won the game. But now the ball is in his court. I need to change it. He's on top of the scoreboard. Shortly after my war with my emotions, I fell asleep.

The next day I go about my daily routine. The afternoon hits and I get a phone call. "Are you ready for lunch?" I and my inner emotions are at war again. "Yes, what time shall I expect you?" In about an hour, he says. Ok, it is game time.

We meet up and of course, I look chicly ravishing and he does as well. We go for a drive out of the city. He started out driving and was driving too slow for me. So I asked him to pull over so that I could drive. Driving calms my nerves down, but he didn't know that.

However, he was very quiet. I think he was having a war with his inner self as well. So here I go popping off at the mouth. I'm like; I know we are not going to sit in silence the entire ride. He says, "No, I'm nervous around you and don't want to mess this up." So I said, "start talking or it is about to be ruined." When really my inner self has the biggest grin and totally elated by the comment. Lord, I'm in trouble.

We finally pull up to the restaurant. We get in, seated and order the food. But we don't eat, we continue talking. As we sit there, we become so engrossed with the conversation and each other until the time just passes away. We pack up and head back to the city.

The ride home was extremely melancholy. We didn't say much to each other. I was having another war with my inner self. I was trying to make sense of it all.

He asked if he could call me sometimes. I said ok. I'm thinking a little conversation won't hurt. What's the worst that could happen?

The next morning, I receive a phone call, "Hello Beautiful."
Immediately a war begins with my inner self, "Hello Yourself", I
say. So we go on chatting and never missing a beat with anything.
He's at work and I am as well. But we are still talking. We didn't
want to hang up with each other. We spend several hours a day on
the phone. The conversations we have are never dull and boring.

We would go on like this for several weeks. However, other
feelings start to rise and my inner self and I were at odds with each
other. Lord, I'm about to fall off my wheel.

We finally get a chance to meet for lunch date because of our
hectic schedules. He is surprising me this time. So I am not in
control and my inner self is not happy with that. But I go on with it.
We go grab a bite to eat, walk and talk in the park feeding ducks.
I'm in trouble because the simplicity of it all is turning me on. I
don't say anything, but if he does it's so on. And so it was. But it
was quite different because there wasn't any physical contact, it was
all mental intercourse.

On the ride home, I was extremely quiet. We both were. We
had crossed the lines. The very thing we talked about not doing, we
did. My inner self was growling at me. I couldn't say anything. I was
in shock. What did I just do? However, the sad but touching truth
was I enjoyed every last minute of it.

My inner self went on fighting with me about the idea. Days would go by and we would avoid that subject. But I wanted more. So I approached him with it.

I even made a contract and had him to sign it. The contract merely stated that he would give me all of the mental sexual activity that I wanted, when and where I wanted. It also stated that no one else would be allowed in our circle. I was truly hoping that he would think that I was crazy and not want to deal with me. I was dead wrong. He was totally excited by the idea and signed on the dotted line.

I wake up every morning to his phone calls, long conversations and lunch dates. It's time to go to the next level. He can't get enough of me and I can't get enough of him.

I am enjoying myself. This is a feeling that I haven't felt in a long time. Oh Lord, I'm falling deeper and deeper.

I quickly learned of the affair that I was having in mind thinking why can't I have this for real. I would sit and daydream of these fantasies wishing and hoping that they were real. I used to have this. What happened? I became bitter. But I realized that I didn't want another relationship to fail. I knew that if I wanted the marriage to work, I needed to go to work.

But wait, I still want this illustrious illusion of mine. I'm that type of person and I want it from my husband so he needs to get on board. I don't eat mashed potatoes and gravy everyday and my marriage shouldn't be like that either.

**Rule of Thumb:** This is for men and women; don't think because you show up naked to the party that one or the other is supposed to be turned on. It doesn't work like that.

For Men: Sex is more of a physical emotion.

For Women: Sex is more of a mental emotion.

But in a marriage, there has to be a medium if not, then the other party is not being satisfied.

I need to take control of my mind and my husband of his. Give me all of you and I shall and will do the same. We quickly became new creatures in Christ. Backsliding was and is a thing of the past.

Father, forgive me for I have sinned and I repent. Cheating is not just a physical thing it is also mental.

**Rule of Thumb:** Pray through it; don't try to fix it ourselves. Lean on the Lord. Ask the Lord for patience and humbleness. Learn to lay hands on your own situation. There is no need to run tell everyone because you may end up getting the WRONG input from others. Listen and wait on the Lord.

"Marriage is a marathon, not the 100 yard dash... pace yourself to get to the finish line." The Refresher

We can sometimes start off too rapidly and will tire quickly and have lack of energy to complete the task. Learn to slow it down.

James 1:19 Understand this, my dear brothers and sisters: You must all be quick to listen, slow to speak, and slow to get angry.

My husband knows about the encounter and he has forgiven me. He was appalled by the way it was written, but knows that I am vividly candid and didn't want to sugar coat things. This is not a fairy tale. A life like this happens in the everyday world. We were just brave enough to share our testimony.

This is why I teach on mental connections because I know what they can lead to. If a spouse is covered mentally then it would be hard for them to cheat physically. Find out the problem and fix it.

The writing of my books has been extremely therapeutic for the both of us. True healing and phenomenal strength of both parts is a true blessing from God.

I want the Lord in my life. I was a backslider. I know that I can't straddle the fence. It is a daily struggle, but I remain eager to please God. There is a resting place with my name on it and it isn't Hell. I started to leave him several times, but divorce is not of God. It is always easier to rather than to stay. Everything is not going to be perfect every day.

My husband and I are rebuilding our lives mentally, spiritually, emotionally and physically. We have learned each other's love language and we now know how to love each other. Catering to each other in your specific love language will help the connection grow stronger every day.

"Relationships are like smart phones they need updating and recharging every day." The Refresher

This means constant communicating and reconnecting. Simple text messages through the day, encouraging, motivating and actually enjoying each other's company. Tell your mate how you feel daily because you don't know the day or hour when their or your time is up.

Now I am longing to see him. It is like we are dating again. There is nothing that he couldn't ask me to do that is not already done. When your order is right and you are obedient to the Lord, greater prosperity/blessings are placed on your life.

Try not to allow your marriages to become routine. It was a chase to get it and it is a chase to keep it. My husband really knows what the meaning of the bed is undefiled means! Keep it extra spicy for your mate. No one wants mash potatoes and gravy every day. Even if it is your favorite, you still don't want that every day. Be spontaneous and different in places, encounters or role play.

# God's Angel

The Lord placed yet another mentor in my life. I was hesitant because all of my past mentors left. Everyone needs someone tangible to hold them accountable for their actions. I didn't have the evidence of speaking in other tongues. At first, I really didn't desire to have it. But this new journey, we are on (my husband and I), we need power from the Lord. So one Sunday after church, a sister in Christ (my bestie) came up to me and said "You need power". I gave her one of my famous brow and perched lipped looks and said "I know." Later that night we called the spiritual mentor, she gave directives which were: too fast & pray and she also said we will tarry with you on Thursday. I was like, this is coming rather swiftly. The spiritual mentor and my sister in Christ (my bestie) came to my house, prayed with me and I received the gift of other tongues in literally five minutes.

So a week later my youngest son comes to me and says "Mommy, I want to pray like that, I want to be closer to God" I began to speak in tongues on that note. So that Thursday again, my spiritual mentor, my sister in Christ (my bestie) and I tarried with him. He received the gift of other tongues within five minutes. When everyone left and we (the youngest boy and I) were recapping on what happened, the oldest boy came into the room. My youngest son asked his brother "why don't you want to pray like us, he said I do." So we (the youngest son and I) began to pray with the oldest son and he received within five minutes. We pray together in Holy Spirit daily. Thank You Lord.

I began praying in the Holy Spirit daily. My spiritual mentor formed a "Praying Diva" line, which is a group of ladies that pray every morning before the day starts. She (spiritual mentor) with the guidance of the Holy Spirit selected the ladies who would be on the call. We pray at 6am, 9am, 12pm, 3pm, and 6pm. In the beginning I was like that is a lot, but when you are going through something you want God to show up right then and there. I just figured that I will praise him on credit because my strongholds are broken and breakthroughs are right around the corner. I also felt like if I am getting closer to God than I can't be me. I quickly found out that I had to decrease in order for God to increase in me.

I know now why people have to leave you because where the Lord is about to take you everyone cannot go. My prayer life has truly changed. The way that I look at situations has truly changed because I look at them with my spiritual eyes. I truly thank God for sending her my way.

Proverbs 12:1 Whoever loves discipline loves knowledge, but whoever hates correction is stupid.

**Rule of Thumb**: You are never too high up to receive discipline. God can use anybody to send a message. All you have to do is listen and spiritually discern things that are coming your way.

We must also note that going to church alone won't get you into heaven. Repent daily and forgive others. Don't carry around the pain. There is power in HIS name.

As God is elevating your life, there will be spiritual test that will come about. Anyone can be used in the wake of the test. Be sure to pass it or you will repeat it until you do. Learn to challenge your leaders because sometimes they are wrong. Scriptures and other things can be misinterpreted. Seek God for yourself.

My spiritual mentor saw greatness on my life. She wouldn't allow me to settle for mediocrity. I would often think that she was picking on me. At every turn I was being reprimanded for something or another. She came to me after MAKING me give my first message and said "I am and will always be harder on you because I see it all over you and I will make sure you get what God has for your life."

Patience: "I'm grooming you for Greatness"

The Refresher

Have patience while God is working with you. You are not always going to like your process, but will enjoy your progress. I am truly grateful for that. The test is not always easy and you will want to quit at every turn, but the hard work will pay off. Anything worth having is worth putting in work for.

When the devil comes to attack you, that means that he is mad because you are lining up with the word of God and will try anything to get you back on Team Hell. Keep pressing and moving on until the manifestation comes.@ Team Heaven.

# Striving for Excellence

When God is grooming your life for something, stress, strife and adversity will come along. This may be something in your future or something from your past coming to remind you of where you've come from. Always remember your past doesn't determine your future.

I began enhancing my career choices and going back to school, obtaining numerous degrees and diplomas. I can remember another college graduation, I was thinking that this time would be different. I had a massive graduation dinner and invited my parents. Of course my mother didn't show and my father said that he had to work. I didn't take no for an answer. I drafted him a letter letting him exactly how I felt. Needless to say, he didn't make it to the graduation, but he came by my house the next day. We are rebuilding our relationship now. Although we can't get back those missed years, we can create new years and memories together.

We all spend time together now. It is a wonderful gift for me because I always wanted to have that close knitted family where we would be together on holidays because that's somewhat how it was for me until things shifted.

I've had folks to ask me how can you encourage people about happy relationships and several of yours were torn to shreds. Or what are your credentials? I simply tell them God allowed my life to be a total mess, so that I can encourage the masses on to how rebuild, restore and retain the gifts that God has given them.


It is as simple as this:

What is in your luggage? For years I had hurt, manipulation, unforgiveness, anger, envy, self-righteousness and bitterness all in one bag. And I begin to fill that bag as I went through life never dumping any of it out. So as I picked up another relationship, I picked another bad emotion, never letting go. So when adversity came along I wasn't prepared to put anything else in my bag because it was already full. I said all of that to bring you this message "Empty your luggage!" Don't carry all that stuff around, get rid of it. For it is too heavy. The Holy Spirit, patience and healing should always be kept in your bag at all times. Stop carrying miscellaneous items and people that you don't need and that goes for people as well.

The Refresher

On my quest to strive for excellence and to figure out what God's holy plan for my life was. I was told to write a book of my life. I'm like my life really isn't all that interesting. I knew I was good at writing poems. So at first I decided to only write a book of poems and then my bestie said that I need an explanation to go along with the poems because people are going to want more.

So I was obedient and began to write. Before I knew it, I had written my first book "The Refresher's Course" in a week's time. I knew that I had a story. What I didn't know was that people wanted to hear it.

Originally I designed "The Refresher Course" just goofing around with some associates. It was just suppose to be a course for learning how to be more sexual in your marriage. I figured I could talk about something that I had a vast knowledge of "SEX". But God said different. He was sending people my way to ask me all of these relationship questions and seeking advice from me on the matter. I would tell them the truth, whether they wanted to hear it or not. I've lost so-called friends for telling the truth, but God said the truth will set you free. Not knowing what I was doing for fun, he was getting ready to re-vamp the entire thing into what he wanted it to be. I operate directly under His anointing when giving course advice. I teach couples how to have mental intercourse as well as pointers on the physical side.

You have the "Greatest Source of Power tap into that… I hang around in it."
The Refresher

So every morning that I rise I thank God for it. Then I start naming out all of the great expectations that I have for that day, thanking and praising God in advance for them.

"You can change your circumstances by changing your way of thinking"
The Refresher

Think positively all day, even when negativity shows up. Once your way of thinking changes, then you become unstoppable in your expectations because you are striving for excellence and not taking a "No" for an answer. Sometimes you are put to the test to see how hungry you are for it. Pass your test and Strive for Excellence!

# Sibling Rivalry?

In my darkest hour when I feel as though I may need an unsolicited opinion from my siblings. I can't call on my sister or my brother and it hurts me. We don't have that type of relationship and my boys ask for them, where they are and can I go stay with them. They don't have a connection with their immediate cousins. So here I go making excuses again.  But the truth of the matter is I can't really say that I even know them. We've been out of touch with each other for years and I've tried to reconnect with them but it doesn't last.  It tends to become fake and I don't do that pretend stuff well.

I really feel as though this is a generational curse on our family and it has to end somewhere, why not with us.

The Refresher

My brother would call me every two weeks for money while he was in jail and then even asked me to take care of his daughter. Now when he contacted me with the news of a baby girl, I knew the lifestyle that he and the child's mother were living at the time, I asked them both to allow me to take her and raise her with the boys. I,  with all of my mess didn't want to see a child being shifted from house to house and pillow to post.  My inner self strategically remembered that conversation. My offer was declined. Needless to say I do what I can.  But he is out now and I haven't heard from him.

My sister on the other hand needs the help and won't accept it. So I've learned to pray on situations and keep moving.

It's strange that the majority of my friends and associates laughs at me because they think that I have a phantom family. Holidays used to be real hard for me, but I have learned to create my own traditions with what I have.

I recently looked up my $2^{nd}$ immediate family on Facebook and my findings were quite shocking. My mother looked tired and stressed, my brother, who was conveniently sitting in a prison-made chair with pants hanging below his waist, a mean-mug and his arms folded and my sister, who keeps eating her emotions and gaining weight. Then I took a look at one of my pictures and I just began to do a praise break right then. That could have been me. I saw better and wanted better. I realize that the struggles that I've had made me into a great non-fictional story-filled person with the mind-set to conquer the world and will not allow the world to conquer me.

I have overcome the limits that were set by man and I am still climbing up the ranks to reach the limits set by God!
The Refresher

# Final Thoughts

If I can help one person to make the right decisions in life, then I've, in my book, conquered the world. I just want young people to know that despite all obstacles there is hope for your life. Learn not to lean unto your own understanding but lean on God. Seek his face and guidance for your life. He will place several people in your path to take you to your next level of where he wants you to be. He did it for me and he can and will do the same for you.

Your ultimate goal in life should be to carry out God's holy plan and purpose for your life. Pray on it and he will show it to you. It is never too late to trust or follow him.

**Rule of Thumb:** Know your self's worth. Value YOU because if you don't no one else will.

Several people have to come to me implying that the book shouldn't have been written because too much was said. I just simply responded with this was a project from God, I am on the highway of pleasing him and picking up the saints and sinners who want to undergo a transformation along the way – as far as the message being too much, well the problem with today's society is that we are not saying enough of the right thing. We want to be on the highway of pleasing man, sweeping secrets under the rug and sugar coating the truth.

The message in my books may not be for everyone, but if you look beyond the messiness, you'll find a real heartfelt and needed message. Thank you for taking the time to read my materials.

If there is ever a need to be refreshed, The Refresher is here to help. I can be reached at therefreshercourse@yahoo.com

# Refresher's Poems

To be refreshed is a tall glass of water on a summer's day,

A nice gesture or something warm to say,

With life's struggles, heartache and pain will come,

But just remember the most high, "The Great One"

We can do all things if we just trust and believe.

He gives us wisdom; all we have to do is read,

By taking this journey you will see

Just how good the Lord has been to me.

A wayward soul just out here in the world

No shame, no fear just in constant turmoil

But to be refreshed is not a thing of my past,

But I thank God that all of my chains are broken at last.

### *The College Graduate*

A misguided daughter, a young single mother, a homeless person, a

college graduate full of pain,

I wish we could have that mother/daughter relationship again,

but you decided to take that away,

when you left and I was forced to learn and start my own ways,

but after all, I am still stuck carrying this pain,

Having to be touched by men that I don't even like.

Just to feed the kids and have the necessary things of life.

I tried to bypass it for years.

Now it's all back to haunt me again

Did you ever wonder?

Do you still care?

Did you ever shed any tears,

I didn't I was forced into being strong,

that's how I've learned to move on,

I wish I could turn back time,

and make you stop, make you listen,

and make you see,

exactly what you've missed out on in life with the boys and me.

You turned me into a heartless soul,

No caring, non-sharing emotionless and so cold

Through lots of prayer and people that helped me along the way,

I figured things out, became successful, learn to how to love and

flew straight.

I'm glad that I didn't turn out to be bitter person

And those generational curses let me be the first to break one of
them,
I will love my kids no matter how upsetting they can be,
God placed them here, to enhance my testimony,
Life is just too short to hold grudges and pretend that things didn't
happen,
So I'm letting you know that, I forgive you with an enclosed caption,
For all of my important dates you've missed, I simply forgive you.
I have survived all obstacles and countless sticky situations.
No tears, and no more pain, no more pretending and no more shame
No love was ever lost because prayer really does change things.

## The Wedding

A woman once locked the door and tossed away the key to her heart,

Only giving about 20 to 40 percent of interest

Then God sent a very patient man that wouldn't part.

He was very fun, loving and extremely persistent

He came into my life and

Persuaded me to change my mind.

Just when I thought that,

Love was completely impossible to find

That is when he held out his hand

And shamelessly proved me wrong

He said "You Love me"

And I have loved you since "Day One"

SoI said "I'm proud to take your last name"

I promise I will not put it to shame.

I've waited almost a lifetime for you.

And I'm trusting in God to guide us through.

I have waited for this special day,

And now in your hand my heart will lay,

I knew right away your love was true,

Because you waited five years for me to say "I do".

So today, as you stand there nervous, sweating and waiting for me,

Just know that our lives are about to be so sweet

Because we've found the gift that makes us complete

So "Here is your Wife to Be"

I promise to be the wife that God's want me to be,

I promise to cook, clean and feed the kids,

I promise to be submissive at times,

I even promise to laugh at your corny jokes,

I love you so much and I am so proud to be in your life,

I now pronounce you man and wife!

## *The Marriage*

Kisses in the morning and breakfast in bed,

Thanking God that we are finally wed!

Romance, special gifts, trips, flowers, cards and candy,

This whole marriage thing is kind of dandy,

Through sickness and health until death do us part.

The wonderful wedded bliss is about to start

I'm so happy to be married at last!

So that I can finally get rid of my dreadful past

Mind-blowing sex two and three times a day,

Please keep this up, Lord I pray!

To be with one person to have and to hold,

So that we might, one day grow wise and old.

Our first big argument, it was bad, I thought that I would die.

You looked at me and said "I'm Sorry, Please don't cry".

We can conquer the world, whatever comes our way

As long as we stick together, everything will be okay,

Cast all of your cares on me.

I'll keep them under my lock and key.

The stresses of the day are all a part of life.

Place them on my shoulders as your loving wife

I could go on like this forever,

Think about leaving him, I could never.

A beautiful, happy, successful couple on top and rising

However on the flip side of things, you'll find it quite surprising

Things don't always look like they appear,

The realities of marriage have set in and I feel like distress and destruction is near.

I love my husband but…

Is this marriage built on a lie or trust?

## *The Pain*

Everything that man could want and still not enough

You chose the road often traveled and found that it was tough

I am a rare and precious jewel, a diamond in the rough

Broken china, promises and misused trust

You wanted a trophy wife

But can you handle that type of life?

Being locked into vows only honored by you

You became complacent, relaxed and avoided the truth

Not having the fulfillment of the marriage that you need

You began to question God, Do I stay? or Do I leave?

I'm trying and I don't want to go astray

Lord, send me a sign or tell me what to say

I want passionate, hard core love making, not just a quick fix

I need and want to feel every part of every inch

The bible tells us that the bed is undefiled

And I have no problem honoring my bedroom vows

I'm smart, beautiful, I cook, I clean, I'm even half way submissive

And trust me I know exactly what to do to get his attention

For every inch of my mind, body and soul that you left uncovered

There are people waiting in the wings to make sure that it is

smothered

Listen the same energy you put into the dating game

Is the same energy it takes to keep me tamed

No one wants to go through life and ponder about infidelity

Keep your mate covered and it won't become your reality

Don't think that you have it all together and don't need any advice

Don't make them choose or have to make the ultimate sacrifice

How much is your happiness worth

The price of another man or woman's girth

I am closing and won't go on and on to make the paper cry

But I'm warning you, don't get linked up with a soul tie

So make sure that you are not sitting around depressed

By keeping your relationships and marriages fully refreshed.

### *The Lord*

Sometimes I feel damaged, discouraged, and depressed.

But I remain determined

At times I feel secluded, saddened, and stressed

But I have strength

I've learned to claim full term breakthroughs, abundant grace and favor

And I have uncompromisable faith

And in my midnight hour, God takes all of my pain away

He told that he would never leave me and never forsake me

And I know this to be the Gospel truth

I must tell you to wait on him because He is no better to me than he can and will be to you

So as I close I will leave you with this

They hung him high and stretched him wide

Just think about it your problems are minute compared to his.

God sits high and he looks low

His grace and mercy will always be shown

Learned to give God, his due diligence time

Because when it is all said and done, you won't be left behind

The Book of Revelations tells us that "It's all coming to an end"

And we don't know the day or hour, but we must contend

I will pray, fast and worship his holy name

So when the manifestation comes, I won't be blamed

And I will go to my true resting place

Because I shall have everlasting favor, peace and grace.

My marriage is not over; God said that it isn't through

That's why he had me bring this message to all of you

Prayer really does work

Thus the reason for The Refresher Course.

# THE REFRESHER'S COURSE

## "Work through it"

### Tonya Woodridge-Jarvis

I am a paralegal by day and a Certified Marriage Educator/author by night. <u>The Refresher's Course</u> was my first book and a snippet of my life's story. I have also developed a course called The Refresher Course, which is to help married couples revitalize their connection. I've always had a passion for helping people and wanted to write my story in high hopes of encouraging someone to pursue their dreams and aspirations no matter what their circumstance/obstacles may be. If you would like to connect with me, follow me on instagram and Facebook @therefreshercourse.

### *I am "The Refresher"*

*Special Thanks to my "Glam Team".*
*You guys are awesome!*
*Trenetta Clark Savage-Style by Tre (Hair)*
*Richelle Washington-Chic by Chelle (Make-up)*
*Christopher Palmer-CPalmer Photography(Picture)*

www.ingramcontent.com/pod-product-compliance
Lightning Source LLC
Chambersburg PA
CBHW040311010626
45792CB00022B/116